City Safari

Squirrel

Isabel Thomas

Heinemann
LIBRARY
Chicago, Illinois

To contact Capstone Global Library please phone 800-747-4992,
or visit our web site www.capstonepub.com

Edited by Dan Nunn, Rebecca Rissman, and Helen Cox
Cannons
Designed by Tim Bond
Original illustrations © Capstone Global Library Ltd 2014
Picture research by Mica Brancic
Production by Helen McCreath
Originated by Capstone Global Library Ltd
Printed and bound in China

17 16 15 14 13
10 9 8 7 6 5 4 3 2 1

Library of Congress Cataloging-in-Publication Data
Thomas, Isabel, 1980- author.
  Squirrel / Isabel Thomas.
    pages cm.—(City safari)
  Includes bibliographical references and index.
  ISBN 978-1-4329-8809-8 (hb)—ISBN 978-1-4329-8816-6 (pb) 1.
Gray squirrel—Juvenile literature. 2. Squirrels—Behavior—Juvenile
literature. 3. Urban animals—Juvenile literature. I. Title.

SB994.S67T46 2014
599.36'2—dc23   2013017409

Acknowledgments
The author and publisher are grateful to the following for
permission to reproduce copyright material: Alamy pp. 11 (©
Dizzy), 14 (© David Mabe), 18 (© Thom Moore), 19 (© Richard
Newton), 23 den (© Dizzy), 23 loft insulation (© Richard Newton),
23 mate (© Thom Moore); FLPA pp. 9 (David Tipling), 13 (Bill
Coster), 15 (Erica Olsen), 17 (Wayne Hutchinson), 21 (S & D & K
Maslowski), 23 predator (Wayne Hutchinson); Getty Images p.
4 (Tim Graham); Naturepl.com pp. 6 inset (© Bruno D'Amicis),
6 main & 7 (both © Warwick Sloss), 10 (© Doug Wechsler), 16
(© Rolf Nussbaumer), 20 (© Andrew Cooper), 23 drey (© Doug
Wechsler); Shutterstock pp. 5 (© ivvv1975) 6 (© Tom Reichner),
8 (© Yannick FEL), 12 (© Paul Orr), 23 fungi (© James Ac), 23
sense (© S.Cooper Digital).

Front cover photograph of a squirrel reproduced with permission
of Shutterstock (© Photomika-com). Back cover photograph of a
squirrel having a meal of bird seed reproduced with permission
of Shutterstock (© Paul Orr).

We would like to thank Michael Bright for his invaluable help in
the preparation of this book.

Warning!

Never touch wild animals
or their homes. Some wild
animals carry diseases.
Scared animals may bite
or scratch you. Never hold
food for a squirrel to eat.
It may bite your finger
by mistake.

Note about spotter icon

Your eyes, ears,
and nose can tell you if a
squirrel is nearby. Look for
these clues as you read the
book, and find out more on
page 22.

Contents

Some words are shown in bold, **like this**.
You can find them in the glossary on page 23.

Who Has Been Spotted Stealing Picnic Food?

Gray fur. Short front legs. A bushy tail. It's a gray squirrel!

Pets are not the only animals that live in towns and cities.

red-brown patches

bushy tail

white belly

short front legs

long claws

Many wild animals like to live near people, too.

Come on a city safari. Find out if squirrels are living near you.

Why Do Squirrels Live in Towns and Cities?

Country squirrels live in woodlands with lots of big trees.

It can be hard for squirrels to find food in cold weather.

Towns and cities are warmer than the country. There are fewer **predators**.

Parks and backyards are full of treetop homes and tasty food.

What Makes Squirrels Good at Living in Towns and Cities?

Gray squirrels are not afraid to look for food near people.

If they **sense** danger, they climb to safety quickly.

Squirrels can climb very well.

Their curved claws grip things, and their tails help them steer as they jump from place to place.

Where Do Squirrels Rest and Sleep

Gray squirrels spend most of their time in trees.

They use leaves and twigs to build round nests called **dreys**.

They also build **dens** in warm places, such as hollow tree trunks and attics.

These high-up nests and dens are safe places to rest and sleep.

What Do Squirrels Eat?

Squirrels use their eyes and nose to find food on the ground.

Their sharp front teeth can crack open nuts, and nibble twigs and pinecones.

Squirrels also like fruit, seeds, buds, insects, bird eggs, and **fungi**.

They remember where to find tasty food, and visit these favorite places every day.

Why Do Squirrels Like Living Near People?

Backyards are full of snacks, such as bulbs, fish, fruit, and birdseed.

City squirrels often find more food than they can eat.

Squirrels dig small holes to bury extra nuts and seeds.

They sniff it out in winter, when there is less food around.

What Dangers Do Squirrels Face in Towns and Cities?

Gray squirrels can damage buildings with their strong teeth.

They can harm trees by tearing off the bark.

Many gray squirrels are trapped by people to stop them from doing damage.

In some places, people also hunt squirrels for food.

When Do Squirrels Have Babies?

Most squirrels **mate** twice a year, in May and December.

Look for males chasing females, making lots of noise!

The female lines a **drey** with soft things, such as moss, grass, paper, or **loft insulation**.

Three or four babies are born in the drey.

Why Is It Hard to Spot a Baby Squirrel?

The mother squirrel looks after her babies inside the **drey**.

After two months, the babies start to play outside, but they stay near the drey.

This makes it very hard to spot a
baby squirrel.

After three months, the young squirrels
leave and build dreys of their own.

Squirrel Spotter's Guide

Look back at the sights, sounds, and smells that tell you a squirrel might be nearby. Use these clues to go on your own city safari.

1 Look for squirrel footprints in mud or snow. Their front feet leave four claw marks, and their back feet leave five claw marks.

2 Try spotting a **drey** in winter, when trees have no leaves. The nests are the size of a football.

3 Squirrels are messy eaters. Look for nibbled shells or pinecones at the bottom of trees.

4 Squirrels make different noises. Listen for a clicking "kuk, kuk, kuk" alarm call, and the chattering sounds of males when it is time to **mate**.

Picture Glossary

 **den** hidden home of a wild animal

 **drey** squirrel's nest

 **fungi** mushrooms and toadstools

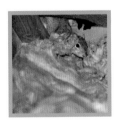 **loft insulation** material put into the loft of a house, to help keep the house warm

 **mate** when a male and female animal get together to have babies

 **predator** animal that hunts other animals for food

 **sense** find out what is around through sight, hearing, smell, taste, and touch

Find Out More

Books

Owen, Ruth. *Squirrel Kits (Wild Baby Animals)*.
   New York: Bearport, 2011.

Zobel, Derek. *Squirrels (Backyard Wildlife)*.
   Minneapolis, Minn.: Bellwether Media, 2011.

Web sites

FactHound offers a safe, fun way to find Internet sites related to this book. All of the sites on FactHound have been researched by our staff.

Here's all you do:
Visit www.facthound.com
Type in this code: 9781432988098

Index